611

CR

Electrifying Eco-Race Cars

by Michael Sandler

Consultant: Mike McNessor
Automotive Journalist

BEARPORT
PUBLISHING

New York, New York

Credits

Cover and Title Page, © Courtesy of Future Vehicle Technologies, Inc.; 4, © Anthony Devlin/Press Association via AP Images; 5, Courtesy of The University of Michigan Solar Car Team/Alex Dowling; 6, © Kathryn LoConte/Thayer School of Engineering at Dartmouth; 7, © Kathryn LoConte/Thayer School of Engineering at Dartmouth; 8, © Markus Hansen/Action Press/ZUMA Press/Newscom; 9, © pbpgalleries/Alamy; 10, Courtesy of Future Vehicle Technologies Inc.; 10-11, Courtesy of Future Vehicle Technologies Inc.; 12, Courtesy of The University of Michigan Solar Car Team/Alex Dowling; 12-13, Courtesy of The University of Michigan Solar Car Team/Alex Dowling; 14-15, © Gary Francis/ZUMA Press/Newscom; 15, © Global Green Challenge/AFP/Getty Images/Newscom; 16, Courtesy of GreenGT Twenty-4; 17, © AP Images/Douglas Rea; 18-19, © CB2/ZOB/WENN/Newscom; 19, © Anthony Devlin/PA Photos/Landov; 20–21, © Barry Hathaway,Courtesy of The Buckeye Bullet team; 21, Courtesy of The Buckeye Bullet team; 22T, © Adrian Dennis/AFP/Getty Images/Newscom; 22B, Courtesy of Edison2.

Publisher: Kenn Goin
Senior Editor: Lisa Wiseman
Creative Director: Spencer Brinker
Design: Debrah Kaiser
Photo Researcher: James O'Connor

Library of Congress Cataloging-in-Publication Data

Sandler, Michael, 1965–
  Electrifying eco–race cars / by Michael Sandler.
    p. cm. — (Fast rides)
  Includes bibliographical references and index.
  ISBN-13: 978-1-61772-137-3 (library binding)
  ISBN-10: 1-61772-137-9 (library binding)
 1. Electric automobiles—Juvenile literature. 2. Automobiles, Racing—Juvenile literature. I. Title.
  TL220.S25 2011
  629.228—dc22

                    2010040095

For more information, write to Bearport Publishing Company, Inc., 101 Fifth Avenue, Suite 6R, New York, New York 10003. Printed in the United States of America in North Mankato, Minnesota.

121510
10810CGB

10 9 8 7 6 5 4 3 2 1

Table of Contents

Eco-Racers

Race cars are known for their amazing speed. Unfortunately, they are also known for not being **eco-friendly**. Most fast automobiles guzzle gas, which is made from **fossil fuels**. Once Earth's supply of fossil fuels is used up, it can't be replaced. Burning these fuels also creates air pollution and releases harmful **greenhouse gases** that contribute to **global warming**. Do all fast cars harm the environment?

The Greenbird, shown here with inventor Richard Jenkins, relies solely on the wind for power.

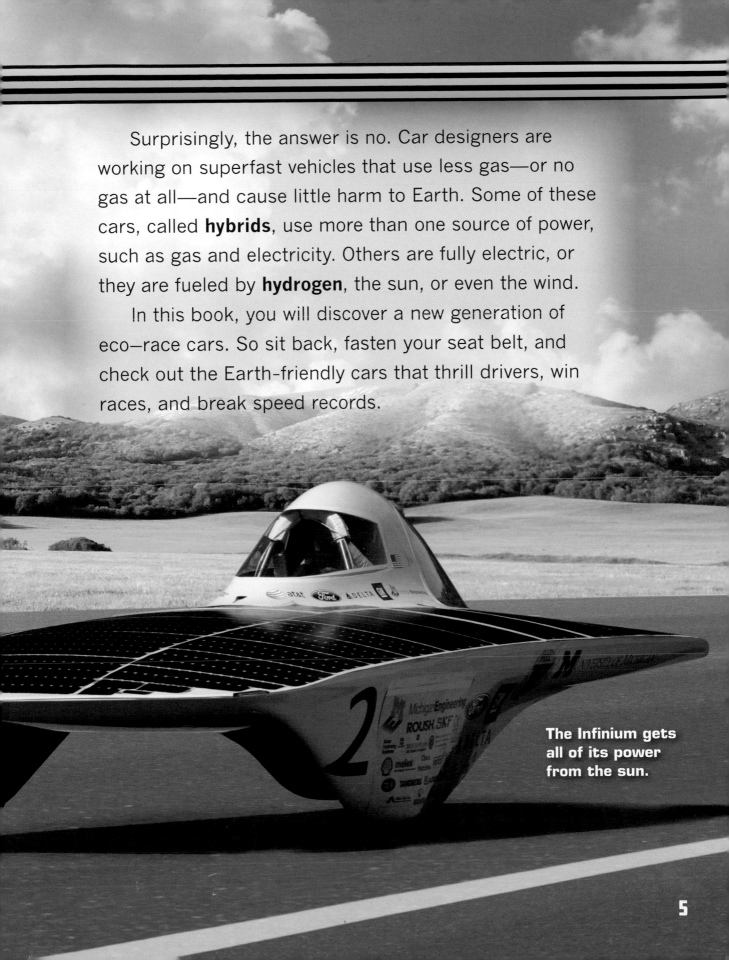

Surprisingly, the answer is no. Car designers are working on superfast vehicles that use less gas—or no gas at all—and cause little harm to Earth. Some of these cars, called **hybrids**, use more than one source of power, such as gas and electricity. Others are fully electric, or they are fueled by **hydrogen**, the sun, or even the wind.

In this book, you will discover a new generation of eco—race cars. So sit back, fasten your seat belt, and check out the Earth-friendly cars that thrill drivers, win races, and break speed records.

The Infinium gets all of its power from the sun.

SquadraCorse

TYPE: Hybrid Gas/Electric **TOP SPEED:** 75 miles per hour (120 kph)
BUILDER: Politecnico di Torino **COUNTRY:** Italy

Where can you find eco-racers? One place is the Formula Hybrid International Competition in New Hampshire. This special racing event is for college students interested in **green technology**. Student teams compete using fast, low-pollution hybrids that they have designed themselves.

The SquadraCorse team works on their car.

In 2010, the SquadraCorse was named the overall best hybrid at the event. Built at a university in Italy, the SquadraCorse is a formula racer—a one-seated car that doesn't have a roof. The car has two power sources—a gasoline engine and an **electric motor**. Hybrids like the SquadraCorse produce much less pollution than those that use gas alone.

The **SquadraCorse racing down the track at the 2010 Formula Hybrid International Competition**

The SquadraCorse's **tight steering**, which lets it weave around obstacles, helped the car take first place in the **autocross** event. This is one of the many contests held at the Formula Hybrid International Competition.

Tesla Roadster

TYPE: Battery electric   **TOP SPEED:** 125 miles per hour (201 kph)
BUILDER: Tesla   **COUNTRY:** United States

Sports cars are similar to race cars as they both go extremely fast. However, sports cars can be driven on regular streets as well as on racetracks. These cars provide quick **acceleration** and high speeds, but most use up a lot of gas. The Tesla Roadster is different. It's a fully electric-powered sports car that doesn't use gas at all.

Instead of stopping at a gas station to fuel up, the Tesla is plugged into an electrical outlet, just like a cell phone. Energy is stored in the car's battery pack. The Tesla can be driven about 240 miles (386 km) before running out of juice.

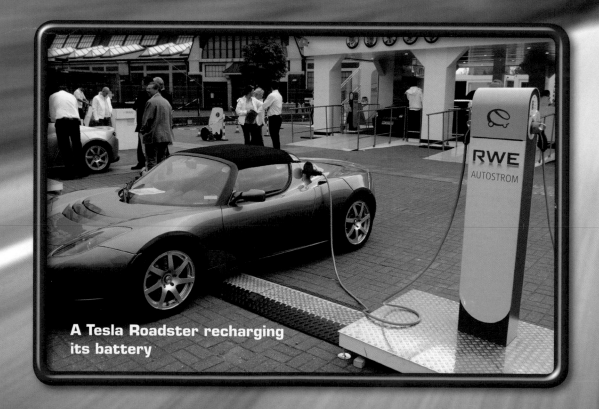

A Tesla Roadster recharging its battery

During those miles, the Tesla proves that eco-friendly vehicles can be true sports cars. When the accelerator is held down, the car reaches 60 miles per hour (97 kph) in less than four seconds. The smooth two-seater is very low to the ground, and its sticky tires grip the road, allowing the Tesla to handle the tightest curves.

As of summer 2010, more than 1,000 Tesla Roadsters had been bought by sports car fans in 25 countries.

eVaro

TYPE: Hybrid Gas/Electric **PROJECTED TOP SPEED:** 135 miles per hour (217 kph)
BUILDER: Future Vehicle Technologies **COUNTRY:** Canada

As more buyers are demanding low-polluting sports cars, more companies are jumping at the chance to make them. One upcoming model is the eVaro hybrid. Most hybrids have a gasoline engine in addition to their electric motors. The eVaro doesn't. Instead, it has a small gas-powered **generator**.

When the batteries that power the eVaro's electric motor run down, the gas-powered generator creates electricity to recharge them. This means that the eVaro doesn't need to be plugged into an electrical outlet to keep moving.

The eVaro has a special door that has to be pulled up to open.

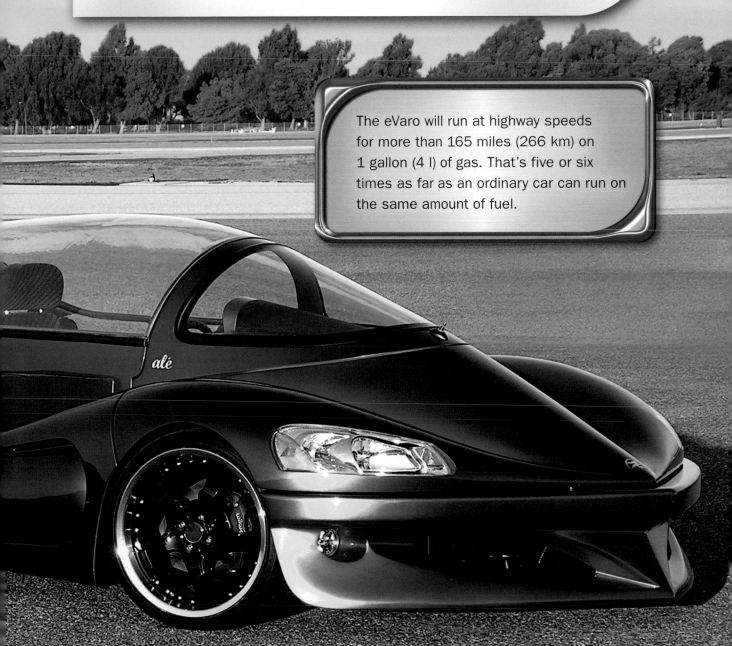

The eVaro's **aerodynamic** teardrop shape and three-wheel design make it extra **fuel efficient**. Most drivers will be able to do a full day's driving without using any gas at all. Less fuel burned means less pollution, but it doesn't mean less fun. The futuristic eVaro will zoom from 0 to 60 miles per hour (0 to 97 kph) in just five seconds.

The eVaro will run at highway speeds for more than 165 miles (266 km) on 1 gallon (4 l) of gas. That's five or six times as far as an ordinary car can run on the same amount of fuel.

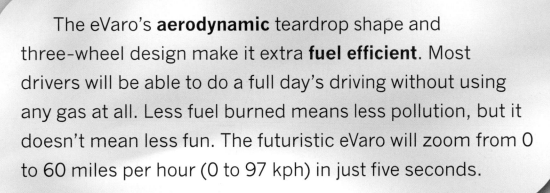

Infinium

TYPE: Solar   **TOP SPEED:** 105 miles per hour (169 kph)
BUILDER: University of Michigan Solar Car Team   **COUNTRY:** United States

Solar power is very friendly to the environment. The sun never runs out of energy, and solar-powered machines don't release greenhouse gases that contribute to global warming. The Infinium—built by Michigan college students—shows how well the sun can power race cars.

The one-passenger racer has a wide, flat surface that contains thousands of **solar cells**, which soak up the sun's rays and convert them to electricity. This electric energy is stored in batteries inside the car. The batteries can power the car's electric motor for about three hours—even when the sun isn't shining.

The University of Michigan Solar Car Team working on the Infinium

In May 2010, the Michigan students took the Infinium to the American Solar Challenge. This race for solar-powered cars, which was 1,100 miles (1,770 km) long, began in Oklahoma and ended in Illinois. The Infinium came in first, ahead of 12 other cars.

The Infinium's motor uses no more energy than a hair dryer.

The Infinium during the American Solar Challenge in 2010

Tokai Challenger

TYPE: Solar   **TOP SPEED:** 94 miles per hour (151 kph)
BUILDER: Tokai University team   **COUNTRY:** Japan

While the Infinium is fast, it does have some competition—the Tokai Challenger. Built by a team of Japanese students and professors, this car proved its abilities in 2009's World Solar Challenge.

This multiple-day race took place in Australia. More than 30 cars drove nearly 2,000 miles (3,219 km) across the country. The Tokai Challenger passed the Infinium on the first day of the **rally** and it never looked back. This super eco-car then went on to win the world's most famous race for solar-powered cars.

The Challenger's special solar cells are what boosted the car to victory. First used to power **space satellites**, they provided maximum use of the hot Australian sun's blazing power.

The Tokai Challenger averaged 63 miles per hour (101 kph) over the course of the four-day race.

Japan's Tokai University team with their solar-powered Tokai Challenger in Australia

The Tokai Challenger races across Australia.

GreenGT Twenty-4

TYPE: Solar electric   **PROJECTED TOP SPEED:** 171 miles per hour (275 kph)
BUILDER: GreenGT   **COUNTRY:** Switzerland

The 24 Hours of Le Mans is one of the world's longest and most famous auto races. On a course near Le Mans, France, teams of drivers try to complete the most laps in a 24-hour period. Naturally, with all that driving, a whole lot of gas is burned. Car builder GreenGT, however, has a plan to race Le Mans in a more eco-friendly way. The company wants to use no gas at all.

The GreenGT Twenty-4

Their car, the GreenGT Twenty-4, is still a **prototype**, but when it's finished, it may be an eco-racing masterpiece. The car will have two electric engines powered by solar cells. The body and frame will be made from ultra-light materials such as **carbon fiber** and **fiberglass**. If the GreenGT Twenty-4 does well, **endurance** racing may become much greener in the future.

The 24 Hours of Le Mans racetrack

GreenGT hopes to produce a version of their car for use on highways and roads as well as on racetracks.

Greenbird

TYPE: Wind   **TOP SPEED:** 126 miles per hour (203 kph)
BUILDER: Richard Jenkins   **COUNTRY:** Great Britain

Can wind power be used to push a car to furious speeds? British inventor Richard Jenkins has proved that it can. He spent ten years designing the Greenbird racer, which looks like a super-high-tech sailboat.

Unlike a boat's fabric sail, the Greenbird's sail is made from light but strong carbon fiber. When this sail catches the wind, it can **propel** the Greenbird to move at very high speeds.

On the morning of March 26, 2009, with the wind gusting strongly, Jenkins "sailed" the Greenbird across a dry lake bed on the border between California and Nevada. Going at 126 miles per hour (203 kph), Jenkins's run set a new land-speed record for wind-powered vehicles.

The Greenbird has no motor. It relies on wind power alone to gain speed.

Richard Jenkins
and his Greenbird

The Greenbird
after breaking the
land-speed record for
wind-powered vehicles

Venturi Buckeye Bullet 2

TYPE: Hydrogen fuel cell   **TOP SPEED:** 303 miles per hour (488 kph)
BUILDER: Ohio State University students   **COUNTRY:** United States

One eco-racer outspeeds all the others. The car is the Venturi Buckeye Bullet 2, designed by students from Ohio State University.

This racer, which is 36 feet (11 m) long, is powered by two fuel cells. These devices use chemicals to generate power—combining oxygen and hydrogen to create electricity. The electricity then feeds a huge 700-**horsepower** motor at the front of the car. The motor creates so much power that the Buckeye Bullet 2 needs to use parachutes when it's time to slow down and stop.

When oxygen and hydrogen mix to create electricity, they also create heat. The Buckeye Bullet 2 is loaded up with ice before each run to keep the car from overheating.

On September 25, 2009, the Buckeye Bullet 2 roared across the Bonneville Salt Flats in Utah at more than 300 miles per hour (483 kph). The Ohio State team's run set a world speed record for hydrogen fuel cell electric-powered vehicles.

The Venturi Buckeye Bullet 2 using a parachute to slow down

The Venturi Buckeye Bullet 2 team and their car

More Eco-Racers

WorldFirst Formula 3

The British WorldFirst F3 is unique among racing cars. Instead of running on gas, it's powered by chocolate! The WorldFirst F3 runs on vegetable oil and leftover waste products from chocolate-making factories! In addition, the car is built from Earth-friendly materials such as potatoes, carrots, and nutshells. The unusual materials don't slow down this racer. The WorldFirst F3 has reached speeds of more than 120 miles per hour (193 kph).

The Edison2 Very Light Car

The Edison2's designers set out to create the most fuel-efficient car ever made! To do so, they kept it simple, using as few parts as possible and keeping them lightweight. A part that weighs one pound (.5 kg) in an ordinary car may weigh just a few ounces in the ultra-aerodynamic Very Light Car. The Edison2 can go 100 miles (161 km) on 1 gallon (4 l) of gasoline!

acceleration (ak-*sel*-uh-RAY-shuhn) the increase of the rate of speed

aerodynamic (*air*-oh-dye-NAM-ik) designed to move quickly through the air

autocross (AW-toh-*krawss*) a timed racing competition in which cars drive around traffic cones placed on a track

carbon fiber (KAR-bun FYE-bur) a material made from thin carbon threads that's very strong but also very light

eco-friendly (*ee*-koh-FREND-lee) something that's not harmful to Earth or the environment

electric motor (i-LEK-trik MOH-tur) a motor that is powered by electricity

endurance (en-DUR-uhnss) the ability to keep going

fiberglass (FYE-bur-*glass*) a strong material made from very fine threads of glass

fossil fuels (FOSS-uhl FYOO-uhlz) fuels such as coal, oil, or natural gas made from the remains of plants and animals that died millions of years ago

fuel efficient (FYOO-uhl uh-FISH-uhnt) able to travel for long distances without using very much fuel

generator (JEN-uh-*ray*-tur) a machine that produces electricity

global warming (GLOHB-uhl WORM-ing) the gradual heating up of Earth's air and water; this is caused by a buildup of greenhouse gases that trap heat from the sun in Earth's atmosphere

greenhouse gases (GREEN-*houss* GAS-iz) carbon dioxide and other gases that trap warm air in Earth's atmosphere so it cannot escape into space

green technology (GREEN tek-NOL-uh-jee) the use of science and engineering to help protect Earth and the environment

horsepower (HORSS-pou-ur) a unit for measuring an engine's power

hybrids (HYE-bridz) cars with two power sources, usually gas and electricity

hydrogen (HYE-druh-juhn) a colorless, odorless gas found in the air

propel (pruh-PEL) to push forward

prototype (PROH-tuh-*tipe*) the first version of an invention; it is created to see if the invention will work properly

rally (RAL-ee) a type of auto race in which cars travel from one point to another rather than around a track

solar cells (SOH-lur SELZ) devices that can change energy from the sun into electrical energy

space satellites (SPAYSS SAT-uh-*lites*) objects put into orbit around Earth to perform tasks such as collecting data or transmitting radio signals

tight steering (TITE STIHR-ing) precise steering that helps a car perform quick, sharp turns

Bibliography

BBC News. "Wind-Powered Car Breaks Record." (March 3, 2009). http://news.bbc.co.uk/2/hi/7968860.stm

The Michigan Daily (University of Michigan)

The New York Times

www.formula-hybrid.org

Read More

Bearce, Stephanie. *All About Electric and Hybrid Cars.* Hockessin, DE: Mitchell Lane (2010).

Doeden, Matt. *Crazy Cars.* Minneapolis, MN: Lerner (2007).

Juettner, Bonnie. *Hybrid Cars.* Chicago: Norwood House Press (2009).

Learn More Online

To learn more about eco-racers, visit
www.bearportpublishing.com/FastRides

Index

About the Author

Brooklyn-based writer Michael Sandler
has written numerous books on sports,
from drag racing to football, for kids and teens.